W9-CBZ-108

H is for Honor

A Military Family Alphabet

Written by Devin Scillian and Illustrated by Victor Juhasz

Sleeping Bear Press™
310 North Main Street, Suite 300
Chelsea, MI 48118
www.sleepingbearpress.com

© 2006 Thomson Gale, a part of the Thomson Corporation.

Thomson, Star Logo and Sleeping Bear Press are trademarks
and Gale is a registered trademark used herein under license.

Printed and bound in China.

First Edition

10 9 8 7 6 5 4 3 2 1

Library of Congress Cataloging-in-Publication Data

Scillian, Devin.
H is for honor : a military family alphabet / written by by Devin Scillian;
illustrated by Victor Juhasz.
p. cm.
Summary: "Using the alphabet format, this picture book describes the many
situations and experiences that military families, especially their children
encounter. For example history, rank, and quarters are explained"—Provided
by publisher.
ISBN 1-58536-292-1
1. United States—Armed Forces—Dictionaries—Handbooks, manuals, etc. 2.
Families of military personnel—Dictionaries—Handbooks, manuals, etc . 3.
Alphabet books—Juvenile literature. I. Juhasz, Victor. II. Title.

UA23.S375 2006
355.00973—dc22   2006008715

For Mom, Dad, Troy, Marty, K.C., Whiskers, & Charlie
—the best family anyone could ask for.

DEVIN

✈

For my son,
LCpl Benjamin Augustus Juhasz, USMC.

VICTOR

Aa

The Armed Services of the United States protect our nation, its people, and its ideals. There are five branches that make up the United States military.

The U.S. Army is the main ground force for the United States. It's the largest and oldest branch of the service, founded in 1775.

The U.S. Air Force is the youngest branch of the service, founded in 1947. The Air Force patrols the sky and space.

The U.S. Navy is the nation's primary sea force. In a world that is mostly water, the Navy patrols and navigates the vast oceans in ships of every size.

Just a few months younger than the Army, the United States Marine Corps also traces its roots to 1775. The Marines are like a bridge between the Army and Navy, able to move between water and land.

As its name implies, the United States Coast Guard guards the coast. The Coast Guard secures the waterways around the borders of the United States.

Give me an A for Army, and an A for Air Force, too.
An A for all the Armed Services behind the red, white, and blue.
They stand at attention, tall and proud, all impeccably dressed.
An A for the American Armed Forces, an A for the world's very best.

The children of military families are often referred to as "military brats." Depending on your parent's branch of service, you might be an "army brat," or a "navy brat," for example. It's not really known where the term "brat" came from. But even though it doesn't sound like a compliment, there is nothing insulting about being called a "military brat."

Boys and girls who grow up in military families have very unique and special childhoods. They tend to move from place to place and attend several schools. But it means having friends all over the world and seeing things that many children never get to see. Sometimes it means going long periods without seeing your mother or father while they are away on duty. That is a sacrifice, and that's why military brats can be proud of their own service to their country.

No offense, but the letter **B** means that you're a brat!
Your brother and your sister, too, and there's nothing wrong with that.
Military kids are known as brats, but far from wild or bad.
They serve their country in their own way just like their mom or dad.

C c

Any Marine will tell you the letter C should stand for Corps.
It takes courage and character. It takes commitment and more.
From Camp Lejeune to Pendleton, the Marine Corps stands by,
ready to go wherever they're called, true to "Semper Fi."

The United States Marine Corps traces its history back to the Revolutionary War. The Continental Congress established the Marines in November of 1775, which means our Marine Corps is actually older than our nation.

The Marines are an *amphibious* force, meaning they can move with ease between land and sea.

Some Marine bases are called "camps," such as Camp Lejeune in North Carolina and Camp Pendleton in California.

The Marine Corps motto is *Semper Fi*, a shortened version of the Latin phrase *semper fidelis*, which means "always faithful."

One of our nation's most famous landmarks is the Iwo Jima Memorial in Washington, D.C. It depicts a group of Marines dramatically raising the American flag after battle in World War II.

Don't you dare dally, and don't be late.
Stand at attention, ramrod straight.
D is the drill sergeant, making things rough.
You'll thank him someday for being so tough.

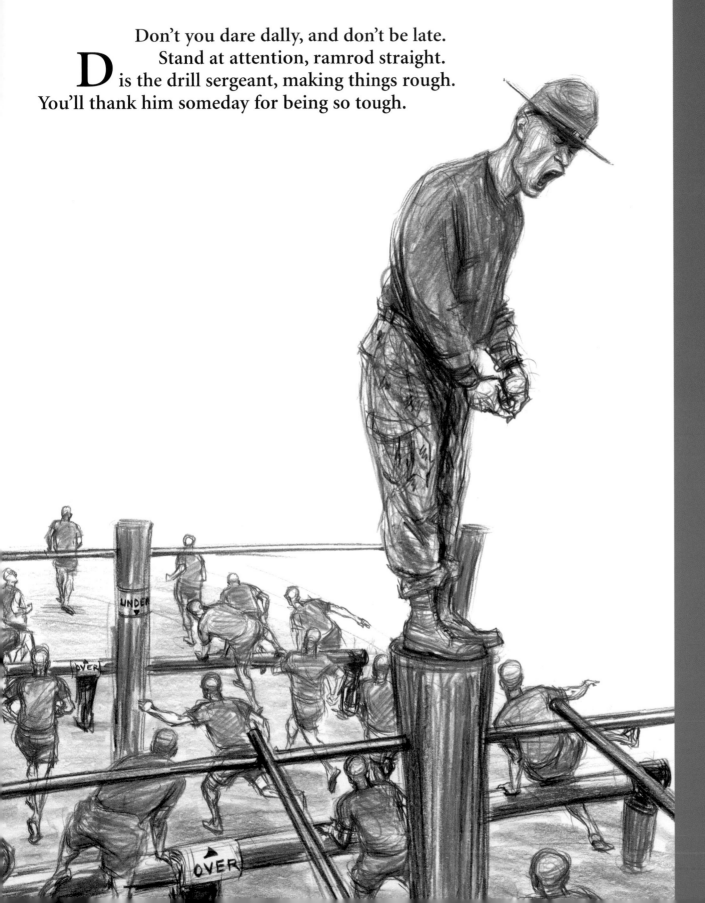

When new recruits report to basic training after joining the military, one of the first people they meet is their drill sergeant. The drill sergeant is a terribly important figure in the life of a recruit. The drill sergeant will see that the recruit learns the basics of military life such as marching in formation, dressing properly in uniform, and following orders.

Movies, television programs, and books have long depicted drill sergeants as tough, loud, ill-tempered men, and many a recruit has hoped for the day when he or she no longer has a drill sergeant to please. But drill sergeants play a terribly important role in creating the military of tomorrow, and many veterans will tell you they owe their lives to the lessons taught them by their drill sergeant.

Dd

The Navy SEALs, the Green Berets, the Army Rangers, of course.
Special Tactics, MEU's, and the daring Delta Force.
E is for the elite force. They're trained with extra care.
They know too well when duty calls danger may be there.

E e

Inside the branches of the military there are smaller forces that specialize in taking on the toughest assignments. Some military assignments seem too risky, too complicated, too secretive, or all three. Those are the missions that can be best accomplished by the elite forces. Members of the elite forces are very highly trained.

The Navy SEALs are a naval unit, but they're hardly limited to the water; SEAL stands for Sea, Air, and Land.

MEU stands for Marine Expeditionary Unit, an elite force within the Marine Corps.

The Green Berets and Army Rangers are two of the elite forces that operate within the U.S. Army.

Combat controllers are an elite group within the Air Force.

Military families are special. Military life can be hectic and unpredictable. Sudden changes halfway around the world can mean that a man or woman in the service may have to leave at a moment's notice for what could be a very long time. Times of war can mean danger and uncertainty. For their families it can mean moving from place to place, or it can mean not seeing a mother or father for months at a time.

The sight of a yellow ribbon wrapped around a tree can be very touching. It means a family is waiting for a loved one to come back home.

Because of the sacrifices they make, military families serve their country in a unique and selfless way.

Behind each sailor, behind each soldier, somebody somewhere cares.
Behind each airman, coastie, and marine someone is saying their prayers.
Wherever Americans fight for freedom they very quickly learn
F's for the families, first and foremost, who wait for their return.

G g

$\mathbf{G}$ is just a game. It's just a game, you say?
Those in the Army and Navy don't quite see it that way.
The Army/Navy football game is a November celebration
of the honor and spirit of those who choose to serve their mighty nation.

The Army/Navy game is a college football game like no other. Every year, the football teams from the United States Military Academy at West Point and the United States Naval Academy from Annapolis face each other late in the college football season. The game is most often held in Philadelphia, which sits roughly between the campuses of the two schools.

Because all of the players are committed to serving in either the Army or Navy after college, many fans see the Army/Navy game as a contest between athletes who play because they love the game and they love their country. At the same time, bragging rights are important to both proud academies.

The game is filled with traditions. At the end of the game, the players stand together, facing the cadets and midshipmen in the stands and sing the academy songs.

From time to time the United States drafts young men and women into the service. But for the most part, the American military is made up of volunteers, young people who believe in their country so much that they wish to wear its uniform.

There is nothing easy about a life in the military, and there are far easier ways to make a living. But fortunately for us, there are many who believe that the American ideals of freedom and equality are worth protecting.

Crispus Attucks is remembered as the first American to give his life in the American Revolution. And in the centuries that have followed, many men and women have made the same sacrifice, honoring the nation that they love.

Those entering the military take an oath of allegiance:

"I do solemnly swear that I will support and defend the Constitution of the United States against all enemies, foreign and domestic; that I will bear true faith and allegiance to the same; that I take this obligation freely, without any mental reservation or purpose of evasion; and that I will well and faithfully discharge the duties of the office on which I am about to enter. So help me God."

Not everyone hears it. It's just a few.
But there's no denying it once you do.
When your country calls, you do your part.
So H is for honor in the American heart.

You're visiting H.Q. to see the C.O. You're surrounded by several officials. You're also surrounded by so many letters, and that's why I's for initials.
R and R, T.D.Y., a night at the B.O.Q.
And when you're hungry it's good to know an M.R.E. will do.

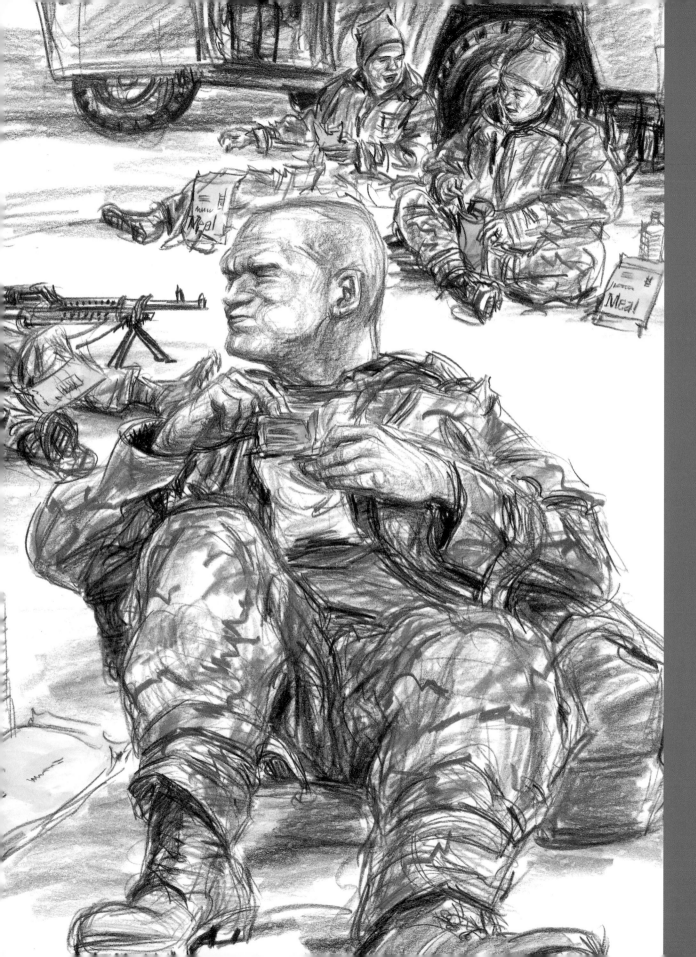

The military likes things to be short and sweet. It has long relied on initials, abbreviations, and acronyms to shorten conversations, radio transmissions, and paperwork. Sometimes a military conversation barely sounds like English! There are hundreds and hundreds of military shortcuts, but with time, most military families find that they become second nature.

M.R.E. stands for "meal ready to eat."
H.Q. means "headquarters."
C.O. refers to "commanding officer."
R and R is short for "rest and relaxation."
T.D.Y. is the abbreviation for "temporary duty."
The B.O.Q. refers to "bachelor officers' quarters."

Ii

Jj

The letter **J** is just the thing to get from here to there.
Here's one racing down the road and there's another up in the air.
Jeeps and jets take different routes, but both of them help prove
the military can't keep still. It's always on the move.

The jeep came into wide use during World War II. It was born when the military needed a lightweight, tough, reliable vehicle that could handle harsh conditions. Jeeps worked so well that other nations quickly developed similar vehicles for their forces.

Jets are the fastest way to fly. The Air Force commands the fastest airplanes in the world. The Navy and Marine Corps can launch jets into the sky from aircraft carriers in the middle of the ocean.

Both jeeps and jets are examples of how military technology can benefit people outside the military. After their introduction into the military, jeeps became popular with thrill-seeking drivers, and now, Jeep is an American brand of vehicle. The mass production of jets began toward the end of World War II, and soon passengers were jetting all over the world.

Few scenes stir the American heart like the sight of a young American returning home safely from overseas, or celebrating a victory in war. World War II was a long and difficult ordeal for the United States. When it finally ended in 1945, a celebration broke out in Times Square in New York City. Photographer Alfred Eisenstaedt snapped a photo of a sweeping kiss shared by an American sailor and an American nurse. The photo appeared in *Life* magazine and was soon seen by people all over the world. It remains to this day a symbol of patriotism and joy, and one of the most famous photographs in American history.

Pucker up for letter K, for a kiss of fabulous flair,
captured in a famous photo on a corner in Times Square.
A happy sailor and a happy gal had learned the war was done.
Their sweeping kiss captured the joy when World War II was won.

L Miles from home, too hot or too cold, lonely for months on end,
arrives in a big green sack. It's the letters that you send.
The leaves are turning, the farm is fine, the puppy keeps chasing his tail.
There's nothing better than getting a letter from home in the bag of mail.

Letters from home can be more precious than gold. The young Americans who join the military are often sent far from home, first for training and then for assignment. For many of them it's the first extended time away from home, and "mail call" can be the best part of the day.

Letters from home are part of a tradition that goes back deep into American history. Many years ago it could take months for a letter to arrive. Today it may be a letter, an e-mail, or a video that brings a glimpse of home across the miles. And those lucky enough to receive a note from home are often expected to share the news, stories, and jokes with their buddies.

Ll

The letter **M** means military police, better known as MPs.
When you live on post or a military base, you'll need a few of these.
They guard the base and keep the place as secure as it can be.
When you arrive at the entrance gate, MPs are the first you see.

Most military installations have their own security units that act as a police force for the base and the families who live there. Military bases, posts, and camps are usually surrounded by fences or borders because they contain a great deal of sensitive information and specialized equipment. The MPs work to make those areas safe and secure.

Traffic through most military bases passes through a guarded gate. Along with policing the training, storage, and housing areas of a base, MPs keep a close eye on those who come and go through the installation's gates.

N n

The United States Navy can trace its beginnings back to the Continental Navy formed during the Revolutionary War. In 1789 our founding fathers ratified the United States Constitution, which included provisions for a naval force to protect our new nation. The U.S. Navy started with six ships, including the U.S.S. *Constitution*. Also known as "Old Ironsides," it's still afloat today.

It may surprise you to learn that the United States Navy actually has many more airplanes than ships. The naval air fleet is the second most powerful in the world, trailing only the United States Air Force. Thus, the U.S. Navy can be miles above sea level in a jet, on the surface of the sea on a ship, or in the darkest recesses of the ocean in a nuclear submarine.

Up in the air in a fighter jet, or down deep in a submarine.
Above the ocean, beneath the sea, and everywhere in between.
We're riding the tide, deep blue and green, constantly churning and wavy.
On ships very small and impossibly large, our N stands for navy.

The letter O Military families tend to move across nations, states, and borders.
means pack your bags for you just got your orders.
Two years here, three years there, your family's on the go.
Your orders mean a brand new part of the world for you to know.

Moving from place to place is a fact of life for most military families. It's not always easy to leave friends or a school that you like. Sometimes, just as the family is starting to feel settled, Mom or Dad comes home and says, "We've got orders," which means it's time to pack up and move again. But there are many advantages to the military lifestyle. Military families get to see much more of the world than other families, often getting the chance to live in a foreign country. Many military kids learn to make new friends very quickly, and as you look at the holiday cards that arrive each year, you realize that you have friends all over the world.

American military bases are spread across the United States and throughout many other countries.

P p

The men and women who make up the United States military are divided into many ranks. Those who are just beginning their careers might be a private in the Army or Marines, an airman in the Air Force, or a seaman in the Navy. Those who have been through officer training can begin as a second lieutenant in the Army, Air Force, and Marines, or an ensign in the Navy.

In any branch of the service, the idea is to move up through the ranks. A second lieutenant may one day become a general and an ensign could climb all the way to the rank of admiral. Each time a new rank is achieved, it's called a promotion, and it's a very proud occasion.

The ranks make up what is known as *the chain of command,* the time-honored way that orders are carried out in the military.

Our letter P will make you proud and cause a little commotion.
Here's a hug and a handshake, too, for P is for promotion.
To move along one rank to the next takes drive and dedication,
so each and every promotion is a cause for celebration.

In the military, your *quarters* refers to your home. Quarters can be the barracks where a new recruit sleeps on a cot, or it can be a large house where a commanding officer and his family live.

Many military bases are large enough to have enormous housing areas of homes, streets, and schools, just like any other American neighborhood. On the oldest bases and forts in the U.S., some of the quarters are very old and living in them can give the family a real sense of history.

Some bases and forts are too small for housing areas. But even if your family lives off-base or off-post, your house can still be referred to as your quarters.

People in the military often talk about working for "Uncle Sam," a nickname for the United States government. (You may notice the United States and Uncle Sam have the same initials!)

Q q

If someone asks about your quarters, I know it may sound funny,
But they'd like to know about your home, not about your money!
Q is for quarters, which means your house, perhaps on government land.
Uncle Sam provides you with quarters, but they won't fit in your hand!

R r

Rise and shine for the letter **R**, early every day.
R is the sound of "Reveille," heard from miles away.
We raise the flag as the bugler plays with the rising of the sun.
He'll play "Retreat" to lower the flag later when day is done.

Using a horn to communicate with soldiers is a practice that goes all the way back to Biblical times. Long before telephones and radios, horns and drums could be used to let troops know when and where to move, when to get up and when to go to bed.

Reveille is a French word meaning "to wake up." *Reveille* is a bright, energetic tune played first thing in the morning to rouse the base or camp.

Retreat is played when the flag is lowered for the day.

The last bugle call of the day is *Taps*. Traditionally, the lights in the barracks should be out by the last note of the song. With its mournful tune, *Taps* is also played at military funerals and can be heard at Arlington National Cemetery every Memorial Day.

The men and women of today's military are part of a long tradition of sacrifice. The freedoms Americans enjoy today are possible because so many were willing to give so much to keep the Stars and Stripes waving as a symbol of liberty and justice.

We rightfully look up to great leaders like George Washington, Abraham Lincoln, and Franklin Roosevelt, but the rich history of freedom in the United States was largely written by the thousands and thousands of men and women who walked away from comfortable lives to stand up for their country. Their legacy survives today in the hearts of those who serve, and in the families of those who stand behind them.

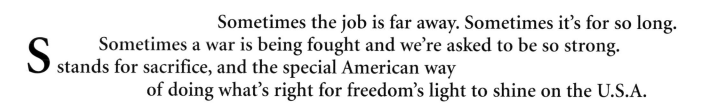

Sometimes the job is far away. Sometimes it's for so long.
Sometimes a war is being fought and we're asked to be so strong.
S stands for sacrifice, and the special American way
of doing what's right for freedom's light to shine on the U.S.A.

Tt

The military is divided into many groups— branches, battalions, wings, divisions, squadrons, companies, and platoons. Each group can be thought of as a team, and from the first day of basic training, the members of the military learn to rely on their teammates.

In an orchestra, it takes many musicians each playing their part to perform a beautiful symphony. The military works the same way. It may appear that a job being performed by a Marine sergeant in California has nothing to do with the work being done by a Navy lieutenant aboard a submarine in the North Atlantic. But by every member of the world-wide team doing their part, the American military carries out its mission of ensuring security for every citizen of the U.S.A.

Whether on a Coast Guard ship or in an Air Force jet,
or an Army tank or a Navy sub, you can certainly bet
that you'll see people work together, busy as they can be.
I think you'll find that teamwork suits us to a T.

Most members of the military wear a uniform for work every day. That uniform can tell you a lot about their rank, what they do, and where they are assigned.

The uniforms of the United States come in many different colors and styles. And each branch has different uniforms for different jobs or occasions. There are uniforms for everything from daily work called *fatigues* to more formal occasions called *dress blues*. The most formal uniform is called *mess dress*.

Patches and ribbons are a part of the uniform, too. They signify the wearer's rank and the honors that have been received. For example, one gold bar on a Navy or Coast Guard uniform means the wearer is an Ensign, while a star on an Army, Air Force, or Marine uniform means you are face to face with a General.

U
u

From army green to desert brown, from white to navy blue, our U stands for uniform, graceful, proud, and true. From a marine's dress blues to a soldier's fatigues, on this we can agree. The uniform of the U.S.A. is a symbol of being free.

V reminds us of all of those who marched these paths before.
Veterans are bound by the gift of service through times of peace and war.
Old and young faces, saluting the flag that waves in the sky above.
All were willing to give their lives for the country that they love.

Every Veterans Day our nation salutes the millions of Americans who have served in the military. Veterans represent different eras, different wars, and different experiences, but they are all bound by the common threads of dedication, sacrifice and honor.

Each time an older veteran passes away, we lose an important connection to our past and to the struggles that have made our modern lives possible.

Veterans Day is observed on November 11, the anniversary of the end of World War I. But other holidays often inspire us to reflect on the importance of the military. Veterans can be celebrated and honored each Memorial Day (the last Monday in May), Flag Day (June 14), and Independence Day (July 4).

For many years if you saw a soldier, you were looking at a "he."
But times have changed, and now that soldier might just be a "she."
So W is for women, defending our nation and lives.
They're All-American mothers, sisters, daughters, and wives.

Even before women joined the military in large numbers, they were extremely important to the nation's armed forces. Dr. Mary Walker received the Medal of Honor in 1865 from President Andrew Johnson for her work as a surgeon during the Civil War. During World War II, "Rosie the Riveter" came to symbolize the many American women who went to work in the factories that produced the equipment and weapons that helped win the war.

But it was in 1917 that Joseph Daniels, the Secretary of the Navy, came to believe there was nothing in the Navy regulations to keep women from serving. Within several months, American women were no longer helping the U.S. military; they were a part of it.

W
W

The letter X stands for exchange, which is where you'll want to stop.
When you live on base or live on post, you'll need a place to shop.
An exchange is a kind of department store with goods from near and far.
It's a PX to some, a BX to others depending on where you are.

Many military bases and forts operate like small towns or cities. They have their own schools, gas stations, and stores. The exchange is like a department store. It's called a BX on an Air Force or Naval base, a PX on an Army post, and an MCX on a Marine installation. (On a Coast Guard base, it's called the CGES.)

Many bases, camps or forts have their own grocery store, too. It's called a *commissary*.

Because the exchange and commissary are considered part of military pay and benefits, only active duty and retired military families can shop there.

X X X

Y is for the reason they do the things they do.
They put their lives on the line and they do it all for YOU.
For you to live a life that's free in a nation proud and strong,
be glad there are those who go to work taking your dreams along.

Y y

The military life isn't for everyone. But everyone *needs* the things that a military can provide. Americans treasure their freedom and the ideals that are put forth in the United States Constitution. But to be able to enjoy and pursue those ideals, Americans must be secure and protected from harm. While we're going to school, watching a movie, or spending time with friends, we sometimes forget that far away, men and women are hard at work making those things possible.

The American military often helps the people of other nations, too, whether it's assisting them in wartime or providing aid and comfort after a natural disaster.

Radio communication is terribly important in the military. It is critical that orders are understood in a very precise way. Misunderstanding a word or number can cause big problems. So the military uses a special phonetic alphabet system for communicating over a radio or phone. A special word stands for each letter.

A—Alpha	N—November
B—Bravo	O—Oscar
C—Charlie	P—Papa
D—Delta	Q—Quebec
E—Echo	R—Romeo
F—Foxtrot	S—Sierra
G—Golf	T—Tango
H—Hotel	U—Uniform
I—India	V—Victor
J—Juliet	W—Whiskey
K—Kilo	X—X-ray
L—Lima	Y—Yankee
M—Mike	Z—Zulu

Z z

Z can stand for Zulu, but as odd as it may sound,
Zulu sometimes stands for Z. It's the other way around!
Zulu for Z, alpha for A, and oscar for the letter O.
The military uses some special words to talk on the radio.

Devin Scillian

Author, musician, and Emmy award-winning broadcast journalist, Devin Scillian grew up the son of a career military officer. His childhood experiences afforded Devin the opportunity to live in more than a dozen places across the U.S. and around the world. Noting that there is nothing insulting about being called a "military brat," Devin reminds us that children in military families are making their own special sacrifices, and that's why military brats can be proud of their service to their country.

Devin now anchors the news for WDIV-TV in Detroit. He and his wife Corey and their four children reside in Grosse Pointe Park, Michigan. Devin has been writing as a broadcast journalist since 1984 and has written several other Sleeping Bear Press titles, including the national bestseller *A is for America: An American Alphabet* and *One Nation: America by the Numbers.*

Victor Juhasz

A graduate of the Parsons School of Design, Victor Juhasz began illustrating in 1974 while still a student and has been working nonstop ever since. His humorous illustrations and caricatures have been commissioned by major magazines, newspapers, advertising agencies, and book publishers both national and international, and his clients include *Time, Newsweek, The New Yorker, Rolling Stone, The New York Times, The Washington Post, GQ*, Oxford University Press, and Warner Books.

Victor lives and works in Stephentown, in the New York Berkshires, with his wife Terri, a psychotherapist. He has three grown sons, Max, Alex, and Ben. *H is for Honor* is his third children's book with Sleeping Bear Press. He is also the illustrator of the popular *D is for Democracy: A Citizen's Alphabet.*